CONNECTIONS

A Leadership Opportunity

ERIK N. BOE

ISBN-13: 978-1516828050
ISBN-10: 1516828054

I dedicate this book to my colleagues who worked with me in the Core Technology Group at Adobe. Their openness and support made it possible to explore, experiment and finally understand how to manage product development using facts. The core of the group is no longer, but the people and the spirit of the group are still at Adobe.

Contents

Preface

Obtaining insight into the belly of a large, dynamic product development organization is difficult. Rarely do you find a system that captures all the information you need to make good decisions. Therefore, questions asked lead to a hunt for data. This takes time and effort. Eventually the number of questions asked overwhelms an organization's ability to gather sufficient data. As a result, decisions are made using old and incomplete data. Access to complete and current data is critical for making good decisions. And without good decisions, the chances of success are poor.

Of all the things you cannot control, access to your own organization's activities should not be among them. Real-time, accurate data beat opinions and speculations every time. And that is what this book is all about— connecting data to create facts that matter.

This is your leadership opportunity.

Acknowledgments

The concept for this book was developed while I was working at Adobe. For years, my colleagues and I collected project data using databases, spreadsheets, and wikis. We finally moved on to design a system to make data collection as simple as possible. Our goal was to provide every user with valuable information that could not be obtained easily elsewhere. The system allowed us to produce data that were current, accurate, and useful. Once it was in place, the management team of the Core Technology Group at Adobe used it to make and to communicate technology investment decisions that impacted the whole company.

I would especially like to thank my then manager, Ranjit Desai, who was immensely supportive during the evolution of this approach.

1

A Leadership Opportunity

What if you had access to data about everything you are currently doing in your company?

What if you had the ability to connect this data to what mattered to you, such as costs, business priorities, and market opportunities?

What if you could apply data about the past and current behavior of your company and of the marketplace to predict outcomes?

What if you could then compare all outcomes to allow you to make decisions to optimize the short- and long-term value of your portfolio of products and technologies?

And what if you could do all of this anytime you wanted without asking anyone to do anything?

Would you do it?

This may not seem possible to implement. Perhaps your thoughts are more along the lines of "Yeah, right." How could you possibly obtain these data without starting a large initiative spanning the whole company? Or, how could you accomplish this without hiring an army of consultants?

By the time you reach the end of this book, I promise you that this sentiment will go away. You will have gained a deeper understanding of how you can leverage what you already have available and of how to build a system to do just this. But before we start, let's take a detour to Alcatraz Island.

Behind the Walls

Imagine it is high noon at the now-closed Alcatraz Federal Penitentiary in San Francisco, California. This maximum-security institution holds some the most dangerous inmates in the country. Guards with loaded rifles are posted in high towers overlooking the island. On one side, San Francisco Bay is covered in fog, but on a clear day you can see the harbor just over a mile away. On the other side, there's a fenced-in concrete yard. Some prisoners are standing in small groups, exchanging stories about the past. Others are walking around savoring their "escape" from their small prison cells. A few are sitting on the steps on one side of the yard—some at the bottom and some halfway up. On the top step sits a lone prisoner leaning back against the wall, enjoying the rays of sunshine reaching down through the fog. He is the boss of the yard. Through the support of his trusted inmates and external connections, he has built a system that creates order in the yard.

Here, everyone knows his place. Each prisoner brings something different to this system. Some are enforcers; they make sure the other inmates follow the rules. Some collect and send messages through their extended networks of prison guards and visitors. Yet others have ways of smuggling in desirable items in exchange for money or favors. Some have connections with guards, who can influence which inmates get selected for the more desirable prison jobs.

Despite this order, there are severe limitations. The ability of prisoners to take action, to make decisions, or to obtain information is limited. The concrete walls separate them from society, where possibilities and information is plentiful and the movement of people creates new opportunities for learning and improvements.

Breaking Down the Walls

Let's return to the present day. Running a large company is like being an inmate in Alcatraz. You live inside your company, separated from the day-to-day bustle of customers. You have your own system. You have a set of rules, communication channels, and the ability to obtain supplies and to make your day the best it can possibly be. Although you are much better off than prisoners, like them you live in a system with indirect and limited connections to the real world. Most everything goes through another person, who adds his or her own interpretation to the information. Only once in a while do you have the ability to leave the walls behind and spend some time in the city.

Securing a meeting with senior leaders in a large corporation is difficult; demands for their time are very high. They employ an administrator to manage their schedule—or to decide who gets on their calendar. A corporation is a very busy place: rarely can leaders spend enough time with customers, investors, internal groups, or individual employees. This makes it difficult for them to understand the best course of action for any one specific challenge or opportunity. Therefore, they are forced to leverage summarized views from a smaller number of groups or people. Seldom do they have access to real-time data that is not filtered or "opinionized." Notwithstanding these obstacles, senior leaders make the best possible decisions and plans based upon what they do have access to. Like the prisoners in Alcatraz, they are held captive—in their own concrete-walled organization.

Some Definitions

There are three definitions that I will use throughout the book, and here I will introduce them before we dive into the details.

Portfolio comes from the Italian word for "carry" and for "sheets" or "leaves" of paper. In the financial world, papers are proof of ownership stocks, bonds, and other securities. In this book, I use portfolio to describe a company's collection of valuables. To be specific, we are talking about people, projects, and products. People and products require no definition. Project, at its core, is a description of a focused effort. In other words, a collection of projects is a company's secret sauce. People, projects, and products are the essential categories of the portfolio of an innovation engine.

Portfolio management is the place where the requirements of customers, partners, and stakeholders come together with product development teams to ensure the creation of roadmaps that have all the right product capabilities at the right time.

Portfolio optimization is used to determine the success, or maximized return achieved, by portfolio management.

Before We Start

This book will teach you how to break down the walls and access real-time information. It will guide you in optimizing your portfolio. But, most importantly, it will change how you think about product development and how you manage the innovation machine. But before we jump into the details, let's take a look at important trends that are changing product development. They will have a significant impact on how you implement portfolio management.

Are you stuck at Alcatraz?

2

Product Development is Going Green

Not long ago, every project was run according to a detailed plan. The plan specified the major milestones that needed to be reached, the tasks that had to be accomplished, and the critical paths that were to be followed in order to estimate a completion date. Before work started in earnest, the project team had to complete a number of documents, such as those outlining marketing requirements, engineering specifications, and test plans. Once the documents were approved and the project funded, the goal was to race to the finish line. This approach is called *waterfall*, which is a sequential process whereby progress is seen as flowing down a path (a waterfall). Along the way, people would be added to compensate for mistakes or changes in requirements. Features would be dropped and quality sacrificed in order to meet milestones. More often than not, the delivery date would be postponed. Once the product was completed, the project team had to quickly prepare a new version to fix all the problems they had not had time to resolve. This cycle would then repeat itself. For every product release, the mountain of technical debt would grow, making it more and more challenging to invest time in developing the features and functions that customers really wanted.

Adding Is Easy

We live in a complex world. There is an ever-increasing amount of information calling our names. We can feel the pressure of presenting and managing this information. There are so many choices to make and problems to solve that it's hard to know where to begin. And sometimes we feel compelled to do it all.

The software industry has exemplified this dilemma for a long time. Every successful product has a list of new capabilities. Adding is easy, but subtracting is not. As a result, many—perhaps most—of these features are rarely used. Over time, this mountain of infrequently employed elements makes it difficult to move ahead. The effort it takes to resolve defects and to move an aging technology onto new platforms makes it hard to take advantage of new technologies and to deliver new features. In addition, it drains project teams, who become stuck in the past.

Subtracting Is Hard

To avoid building "feature mountains" that take years to flatten, the software development industry is leading the change away from planning everything up front. Instead, it is adopting an incremental approach that breaks a product idea or concept into smaller pieces. These pieces are built one by one. Once one piece is completed, it is shown to various customers. The industry wants to know if it adds value: Does the piece have the required functionality? Does it have features that customers want?

This step-by-step approach allows teams to complete a product with minimal technical debt, thereby avoiding the need to constantly ship a newer version to adjust the prior one. A key principle of this approach is that the product is always shippable. Once a minimum set of features has been developed, the first version of the new product can be released and it will work. The next one can then be shipped at any time thereafter. If somebody adds something to a product in development, that piece must be complete. If it destabilizes the product, it cannot be added. The product is not "somewhat complete"—in actuality, it is ready to ship.

It is possible to avoid the feature mountains because the newer pieces are smaller and are delivered more frequently. There is less time to go in a wrong direction. This allows project teams to focus on new innovation and to avoid being distracted by fixing the problems of the current products.

The Green Branch

Evergreens are green forever—not once per year, separated by a long period of hibernation. The "green branch" is a place where every product and component has been fully tested, documented, labeled, and branded and is ready to be shipped. The green branch is the place where each team places its latest fully functional parts, which are released if the benefits of doing so outweigh the costs. It can be a central location or a set of distributed locations that together form the green branch. Either way, products that reach these places are always green, always shippable. This is the foundation for your product portfolio.

This concept is not restricted to software. It can be applied to many different types of deliverables, with some modifications of the time it takes to ship after a unit has been placed into a green branch. It can take only hours to transform software from a shippable state into a product that is actually ready to be released. If you deliver documentation or hardware products, it may take more time. But, as long as there are no surprises from the time a product leaves the green branch and is held in the customer's hands, the concept holds true.

Green Is Growing

Why is this approach becoming popular? The short answer is, because it works. There is a wide range of books and websites that covers this in more detail, so I will touch on it only lightly here. In the industry, the approach— called *agile*—has many flavors, such as *scrum, lean, extreme programing*, and *test-driven development*. Although moving to the agile approach takes a while, once a team gets successful results, they feel empowered and energized. This, in turn, makes for better products.

Seen through a competitive lens, the reason why companies should move toward this approach is that it allows them to react to changes much faster than they ordinarily would. Companies can sometimes respond to market demands within just a few weeks. This, of course, depends upon the product and where it is in its lifecycle.

Another reason for adopting an incremental approach is that it results in better products. The ongoing validation from customers will guide you in the right direction. It is now simpler, faster, and cheaper to reach out to customers than ever before. Why not take advantage of this approach? It can allow you to adjust your product as it is being built and with a higher degree of certainty that once it is ready, customers will love it. In other words, your success rate goes up dramatically.

Is Waterfall All Bad?

Product development is challenging and can be expensive. It requires many different types of specialized skills and demands complicated tools and costly software applications. Because of its complexity and large scope, milestones are placed far into the future, which in turn opens the door for many possible downfalls. I have participated in many waterfall projects, and every one of them faced one or more of the following issues:

- Projects are delivered late, and the bigger they are the higher the risk of delay.
- Many projects ultimately cost more than planned, as measured in weekend work or longer days.
- Quality suffers as teams scurry to meet milestones, creating a large technical debt that forever looms over the ability to invest more in innovation.
- Features are dropped to meet milestones, thereby reducing the value of the product.
- Inefficiencies in development are masked by longer durations in the development milestones. This adds to cost and time pressures.
- It is difficult to make changes to the product late in the development cycle. The world changes constantly. The longer the development cycle, the higher the chance that what is delivered is going to be out of date.
- It is difficult to get customer feedback early in the cycle, as the product is not in a shippable state. Normally, feedback is collected late in the cycle and very little of it has a chance to be included in the product.
- The overhead of coordinating waterfall projects is high, as complicated project plans and dependencies are costly to maintain.

As a result of these experiences, companies feel pain. Employees are on a treadmill that never stops. In this environment, individual heroes are allowed to step in and fix problems or remove barriers. "Tiger teams" are let loose. They are a team of specialists that is brought together to work on a specific problem for a short period of time. Because so much depends upon this one release, every shortcut is open for discussion. Best practices are ignored, and vacations are set aside. The treadmill slows down only after a product ships—and not for long. The mountain of technical debt once again stands in the way of innovation, as the product team almost immediately has to develop a release to fix defects.

But is waterfall all bad? The answer is, no; in many cases it is very appropriate. I would say that the more a project looks like one that has been done before, the better the waterfall approach is. When there is uncertainty about what features a customer wants and likes, however, the approach is less suitable.

The Agile Promise

There are many different agile approaches, but the core premises of all of these are:

- Products are always shippable.
- The time from idea to delivery is shorter.
- Priorities are flexible.
- Transparency is increased.
- Alignment across groups is enhanced.
- Lower technical debt allows more effort to be directed at valuable features.
- Frequent deliveries allow for faster learning and process improvements.

It sounds almost too good to be true, but it works. Results are obtained by allowing small teams to make independent decisions and to deliver value over a short time, typically one to four weeks.

There, are of course, many different ways of becoming more agile, and the results will vary greatly. In addition, the process takes time. With guidance and support, a team can become skilled at using the agile approach in six to nine months. The concepts of the technique are relatively simple, but implementation is not. It takes a dedicated management team, a support group, and someone with prior experience to obtain the best possible outcomes.

In larger corporations, you are faced with making the agile team-focused concept work across many groups and divisions. The concept of "scaled agile" can help. This framework can be learned in less than a week, but it is challenging to implement because it requires a shift in mind-set across the whole organization. It moves the product development model toward an "always-shippable company portfolio," where the decision to ship is about value for the customer versus cost of delivery. The emphasis is no longer about schedule, quality, or scope; it is all about customer value. This change requires a very different approach to project management. A minority of organizations is scaling agile today, but every large company is faced with this decision. How can you make agile work in a large development organization ?

In addition to investing in agile development methodologies, you will need tools and solutions to support you. It is no longer possible to live with testing cycles that require weeks to complete. You cannot endure a software compile-and-build system that has a complex dependency tree and that may only deliver a testable version once per week. It is no longer possible to have a legal team that requires four weeks to review your code for open-source license issues. Your technical documentation team cannot wait until the product is completed to start their work. It is no longer possible to localize software at the end of a cycle. You can no longer wait for patent filings that take months. Nor can you implement a company-wide project planning and approval process with major milestones that span months. And the list goes on. But it is this set of challenges that often prevents a successful transition from waterfall to agile, not the core agile principles.

The Agile Way

Assuming you implemented the agile framework, scaled it across the organization, and improved all your tools and systems, you now have a very different company. Many smaller companies, especially those with Internet-based solutions or hosted services, often start here. Medium-sized and larger organizations often have to transition into this place. But once there, you have a new opportunity in front of you. You can now direct your entire leadership team toward managing your product portfolio in real time.

You have a set of products that are on the market, being used by your customers. You also have a number of projects that are aimed at constantly improving your always-shippable products. The set is not released yet, but can be any time you decide that there is sufficient value for the customer. I am not saying that you have to release a product every day or that you should not plan for a big set of product releases that you want to market in the future. What I am saying is that you can now focus on optimizing your portfolio at a much more granular level than ever before. You can now decide what features will make a difference rather than waiting a long time for a product to ship and hoping that the set of completed features will be enough to make customers happy and to increase revenue. You can also get a request for a new feature though the system much more quickly, as the whole system is set up to respond to change.

Now your organization is spending much more of its time developing features that are deemed to be of higher business value. It is more difficult for lower-impact features to be distributed across products, as the priority of work is closely managed at the feature level with respect to every single project that contributes to the portfolio. Just this step alone will improve development productivity and reduce support cost. The cost goes down because every new feature is scrutinized. No longer are additional "nice to have" features added to the products by developers in dimly light cubicles.

The agile concept is being adopted because it works. Therefore, you can safely assume that your competition either wants to become agile or already has. The decision is not if, but rather when.

Plans Are Still Critical

This change does not mean that you drop product development planning. In fact, there is no conflict here. You should have a vision of the future that includes long-term plans to create products and product lines to grow your company. You should make sure everyone knows what those plans are. Yet, at the same time, expect that plans will change as you learn and as more information becomes available. Better yet, set up the expectation that you will incorporate new learning to make your plans even better.

Volume Versus Value

Once you have prioritized quality and time, it can seem that scope has been sacrificed. In other words, the immediate assumption is that you cannot deliver as much as you perhaps wanted or assumed you could deliver using a different approach. Yes, this might initially seem true if you measure progress using number of features, lines of code, or even number of products. However, are those metrics of customer success? Are consumers looking for more features? More code? More products? Or are they looking for something that works and that adds value to their lives? These questions can lead to a lengthy discussion, with many points of views that will hold true depending upon your particular situation. However, in my experience (having seen this scenario played out hundreds of times), there is no way to win in the long term if your product does not make your customers happy. You can have short-term wins, but they will all come with a cost. Sometimes this might be the right thing to do. But in the long run, value always wins over volume.

Team Versus Individuals

Inventing the future takes time and dedication. Innovation—creating something that has never been done before—is a team sport. A team is fragile; it takes practice to produce great outcomes. Solving a problem and taking on a new challenge is best done by a team, not a collection of individuals.

A constant rotation of team members or reorganizations makes this goal even more challenging. I am not saying that you don't need individuals who have the right skills and experiences. I am not overlooking that when you are building new teams or addressing an emergency, you need to find and assemble the right types of people. But it is a waste of time and energy when the task of assembling new teams or reorganizing becomes the norm—the first path taken for anything new. Instead, the first choice should be deciding who owns the problem or challenge. Once this is determined, find the team and make it a priority for them to address the problem. The second option (if an owner is not found) is to assemble a new team. A team that has worked together for a while and knows how to distribute work has a huge advantage over a group of individuals. A team can get to work faster; they have established roles and responsibilities, and they have a network of support. So, when you can, move work to teams, not individuals to work. A reorganization should be the last alternative.

Bricks and Mortar

How are organizations built? How do you best build teams? It depends upon their skills and what they are capable of getting done. Which individuals are best suited for a particular task? What is their ability to develop new products? Can they localize your products into many languages? Do you have developers who can connect an iPhone application back to your servers? These and many others are the basic questions you must ask about your organization.

The simplest way to address these issues is by using an organizational chart. This gives you some idea about your capabilities. A better approach is to categorize each person's area of expertise. For example, who is a developer, a tester, a localizer, a marketer, and so on? Perhaps you can break this down even further in order to capture the refined skills within a discipline. A developer might be skilled at iPhone application development, while another is a database designer. While these are initial categories, it is important to allow for the fact that developers can learn and migrate their skills into new areas. It is important to not box people into a fixed skill set but to allow them to transition into new areas over time.

A mistake I see leaders routinely make is to look at solving a problem by thinking about developers as "bricks" and ideas as "mortar." You can use any combination to fill a gap—just apply some mortar, and it will come together. There is an assumption that problems are solved via management ingenuity. This view of the world was routine during the Industrial Revolution. All you needed was someone to fill in gap in the assembly line. This simplistic view of the world is obsolete. We live in a complicated world. Each person's ability is different. Inventing the future is about routing the work to a team that is best positioned for the job. Know your organization, know it can change, but don't make it about bricks and mortar. This people information is typically applied when discussing career development and advancements. It is often underutilized when building project teams.

Team Size

A typical problem scenario in developing new products or features is capacity planning. Do we have the right mix of skills to develop a desired set of features? There is nothing more rewarding than knowing that you can find and assign competent people to solve a critical problem for the company. But pursuing capacity as a solution to portfolio management can become a trap. You could end up chasing new people with different skills every time a problem comes up or as a way of meeting the return-on-investment challenge. Set aside the idea of trying to estimate what it takes to get new things done, unless you are an expert on a particular subject. The fact is that most of us are not experts on most of the topics it takes to manage a portfolio.

Since novel ideas are new, nobody knows for sure what it will take to implement them. Just because someone has an important title does not mean that he or she has the answer. It is easy to fall into a trap where, for example, a leader decides that it should take ten people to develop a software-graphic engine. Why should it? Unless you get started and gain more insight, it is difficult to predict.

Instead, step back and let the teams figure out a solution. Let the innovation engine develop and deliver an idea. Let the team sequence the work and build a solution step-by-step. Your job is to look at the results. As a leader, your role is to decide if an investment is worth the return.

Don't consider the size of a team to be the only important factor. Instead, let its ability to produce results guide you. Allow the team itself to request additional members or resources. Give the team the opportunity and time to reach a point at which you can evaluate their results.

The Evolving Role of Leadership

The green branch impacts the responsibilities of company leaders. Before the green branch came to pass, the approach to leadership was to closely monitor milestones and ship dates along the route to the release of a product. Those in charge would constantly move people around to help out with projects that were in trouble. They decided what feature could be dropped in order to meet the ship date, and they would reluctantly ship even if the products did not meet their ideal quality targets. With a green branch, there is no one future ship date to be concerned about; the product is always shippable. There should not be a need to move people around to fix problems. Instead, new feature requests should be moved to the teams, which should be set up to respond to changes that may arise along the way. There should not be a need to sacrifice quality, because every part added to a product must be complete. A product cannot be shipped unless it meets predetermined quality criteria. Of course, something has to give, and it is the scope of a project. There is no longer a fixed plan to ship a specific set of features on a specific day. Instead, there is a prioritized list of features that can ship when ready. Does this lead to fewer features? Perhaps. But the project teams are spending more time on features that matter, and that leads to more valuable products.

This change allows leaders to focus on what they've always wanted to do—to manage product value-add. They get to decide when a collection of features has enough value to justify shipping, transforming from problem-solvers into value optimizers.

Breaking Down the Walls

Begin to think about the company portfolio as being always shippable. This removes the pressure of schedules and instead focuses on adding value. There is no longer a need to gaze into the future. Rather, you can look directly at the current set of products and projects. Every new feature request is an opportunity to add value for a customer. In order to best prioritize features and to take advantage of the company's expertise, look at the company holistically. It is time to step away from optimization within each project. Gather the company product portfolio under one umbrella. Start by breaking down the prison walls and getting real-time access to what is happening across all projects in the company. It is time to leave the prison behind and head for the city.

You can implement many of the concepts in this book using a spreadsheet (despite my negative comments about them in chapter 3). This works for smaller groups with a handful of products. In larger organizations, it becomes more efficient to buy and configure a system. Or you may try to leverage a system you already have and expand it to support portfolio optimization. If you are really brave, you can use the concepts presented to build your own solution. Either way, this book will help you become comfortable living in the city.

Green development is a leadership opportunity—to move from being a problem-solver to being a value optimizer.

3

Project Versus Portfolio Management

What is project management and what is portfolio management? Is it important to make a distinction? Yes! One is about managing projects, while the other is about managing a company.

Before jumping into a discussion of the practical differences, let's take a look at three structures every company is faced with that overlap these two areas. The building blocks of a company's portfolio are products, projects, and people.

These building blocks are organized into three separate structures, each of which has a different purpose. First, we have people who are organized under managers and executives. Every company has an organizational structure composed of leaders, managers, and team members. This is the backbone of the organization, through which a company provides support to enable employees to venture into doing valuable work.

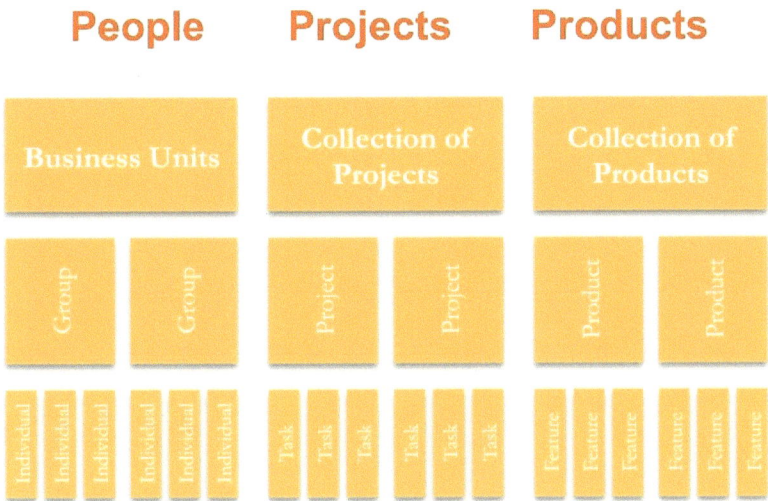

From this springs the need to organize work into projects. A project may have team members from many different groups. Depending upon what is delivered, the makeup of a project team will vary greatly. But, in the end, everyone needs to know what they are responsible for and what tasks are assigned to them. Sometimes the projects are formally named; other times they are not. Either way, work is organized into efforts, or projects.

The product structure often acts as a proxy for the project structure. This is always a bad idea. How a product is created is very different from how it is used. It also makes it impossible to do any kind of investment analysis when a list of products is your project-tracking tool. Therefore, keep the project structure separate from the product structure.

The product structure outlines products and their capabilities, or features. This is what you sell and what a customer buys. A product can have many features or functionalities. Normally, products are grouped into product families because they have similar features or the same customer base.

One Way of Thinking about a Portfolio

In order to build a portfolio management system, the three fundamental elements that need to be managed and connected are people, projects, and products. Without them you cannot gain insight into the impact your portfolio decisions will have. The graphic below captures all of the elements found in project and portfolio management. This is one way of thinking about the three structures. Later on, I will describe a simpler way that is focused on portfolio management.

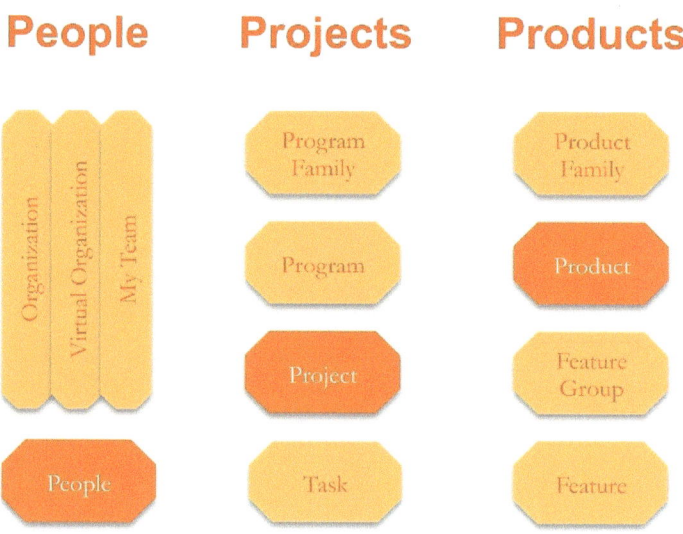

There is one list of people in a company, but how you organize and think about them may change frequently. Projects reflect efforts in the company. They are also fluid; they may be active for just a few weeks or they may last years. There should be one master product list that is kept up-to-date at all times. Let's take a look at each of these structures in more depth.

People

All companies need to have a management structure. This is made up of people who can support us, provide career opportunities, reward us, and help us overcome challenges. In a portfolio management system, the people structure does not advocate that you organize in one way or another. But you need to know who is available to contribute to projects. From an organizational viewpoint, everyone should therefore be listed in the system so that they can be associated with a project.

A fundamental problem of product development organizations is that they do not seem to be able to create a lasting organizational structure to map how work is done. A larger organizational unit is often composed of people from different groups with indirect reporting relationships. Oftentimes specialists such as architects, lawyers, and designers support many different teams at once. This activity is normally not captured in organizational charts. Therefore, it must be displayed in other ways, such as what can be called the *virtual organization*. Having an awareness of these different roles has significant benefits, especially in larger organizations that span many geographical locations. It provides everyone with a way of seeing the extended team in one place and makes it easier to see who is available to work on new projects.

In addition to these two perspectives, there is the view of the local team. If I am a manager of a smaller group, I will most likely rely on the support of many individuals across the virtual organization. Making my team knowledgeable about these players makes it easier for me to identify my scope of influence, connect with the people I actually work with, and get help to complete my deliverables.

The main reason for having different views of various people is to make it easier to find and connect individuals to the portfolio management system—specifically, to connect a person to a project. This is a way of abstracting the organizational structure away from how you manage projects and develop products. There is no need to change the organization just because of portfolio management. Over time, the organization may transform to better support your desired program structure.

Projects

A project is an effort big enough to be given a name. It has a purpose and sets out to bring about change. It can have a start date and an end date, or it can be more of an ongoing effort. Someone leads or owns it. Anyone can create a project to reflect his or her contribution to the company.

In a product development organization, we typically think of the core development team as being an integral part of a project. But there are efforts and people across the whole company that contribute in some way to making a product a reality. These can be supporting groups such as localization, legal, and shipping. They can also be departments such as human resources, as they provide support to the organization to make sure the development groups are functioning. How many types of projects you want to include in portfolio management is up to you. The more complete picture of product cost you are looking for, the more project types should be included.

There is a need to group together projects or efforts that are similar in some way. A collection of projects is called a program. A program has the same governance structure, the same support teams, and a number of projects that are alike or that have many interdependencies. If needed, programs can be organized under program families. These are typically aligned with business units or larger independent groups.

What is your current list of projects? What are people working on? What are they trying to achieve? These questions are important because their answers will enable you to decipher the cost of developing and supporting a product. And this, of course, is necessary when you start comparing investments and returns. In addition, it influences the foundation on which the current and future direction of the company rests. Yet this is an area where most companies struggle.

The people and project questions are often posed before annual planning, a reorganization, or, worse, a layoff (a more neutral term is *reduction in force*). But equally as important is knowing when this question is not asked. Typically, it is not asked when the company is growing and making money. At such times, anyone who has a plausible argument for adding more employees will be heard. The question is also not asked when looking at what part of a product is more frequently used than others. In other words, which features should be invested in and which should be retired.

In either case, creating, maintaining, and getting access to projects and the people who are working on them is, in concept, very easy. But in larger organizations, this is probably one of the most difficult things to do. There are tools that promise to help you, and in larger corporations many of them are often used. Getting data out and compiling it into one list is not easy, but it can be done. A large number of these tools focus on project management and, as such, require a significant investment of time in setting up an enterprise and maintaining the data.

Project tools track schedules. They also track time for various tasks, and that is where things break down. People hate tracking time; they avoid it at all costs. If you use a project tool that requires everyone in the company to log their time against tasks, you have a problem. You may get somewhat useful data when compensation is directly linked to reporting hours, but that is not common in development organizations.

It is worth noting that agile development calls for using time to help teams improve their own predictability in estimating task size. However, this time data is not meant for consumption outside of the team. The predictability of delivery is what matters and is what should be shared with other project teams or managers. Also, agile time tracking is focused on the hours a person has available to contribute directly to a project on a weekly basis. Therefore, it does not include all efforts or functions needed to support an organization in delivering a product.

Regardless, when it comes to more broadly tracking time or people's effort, the default solution is often to use spreadsheets. This tool makes it easy to structure what you want, but collecting the data and maintaining it is very, very time-consuming. The worst use of spreadsheets is to place them online and require everyone to update a particular section or row. In no time, this leads to total chaos.

Wikis, websites that allows collaborative editing online, are also frequently used. They make it easy to capture data and to share it across the whole organization. But they are only slightly better than spreadsheets in terms of usability. In addition, wikis require effort to maintain and may be difficult to connect to other data sources.

Some organizations create their own tools to track projects and people. Oftentimes these are not project management tools, but rather a list of projects that indicates who is working on them. The finance department of a company normally sponsors these tools and uses them to report the costs of product development. They may also use them for tax-credit purposes.

However, these tools are of little value to the people who enter the data and, therefore, yield very inaccurate results. As nobody outside finance finds them useful, they are updated infrequently. And they are typically not linked to any other tool, making product correlations difficult. Despite the many tools and ways in which data can be collected, the results are poor. A company can easily end up with inaccurate and stale information about projects and who is working on them.

Regardless of the challenges, keeping track of projects and the people who are involved in them is important. It is also critical to keep information up-to-date. Not doing so makes it impossible to get a handle on what is taking place in the organization and to proceed on to portfolio management or portfolio optimization.

Products

Product is what the customers see. This is what the company delivers to users. It can be an item that is shipped in a box, services that are delivered, or something else. Regardless of the form it takes, a company must have a master list of its offerings. Creating one list is not easy because of the sometimes-convoluted ways in which products and services are developed, released, upgraded, and sold. A stock-keeping unit (a product or service's identification code) is a way of tracking what is sold. This can be insufficient when dealing with software services, as they are often bundled in different ways. Regardless, it is important to agree upon the creation of a master list of products that can be used across the company as a base for portfolio management.

The product structure is built around features that are organized into feature groups. There can be several levels of features, but in this book I will not delve into more than one level because in most cases the first level is sufficient for portfolio management. Most products are grouped into product families according to their similarity in functionality or customer base. There is often a close correlation between program families and product families. In other words, one program family is frequently responsible for delivering products for a specific product family.

If you want to manage your organization, you need to know your products. This task brings the same challenges as those involving projects and people. Although it seems easy on the surface, in a large organization this task can be difficult to accomplish. It is not enough to refer to a price list. It is not enough to ask every group to send you their latest list. You need to develop a definitive master list of products and features. This is the core of your business. This list is what brings value to your customers and money to the bottom line. It must be up-to-date and accessible to all. What products—or perhaps even as important, what features of a product—are the most valuable for a customer and therefore the ones you should invest in? What features should you leave as is or perhaps remove? This is the holy grail of product development. You may not have the answer today, but having a product master list is a necessary starting point.

Project Management—Below the Line

Delivering a product requires planning and coordination. It requires project management. How that is accomplished will vary. One core aspect of agile development is getting things done in a predictable manner, and as such I see it as a way of managing projects. Project management is centered on getting tasks completed so that features can be delivered. Features are grouped and shipped under a product label. But most of the effort is directed toward who and what. It is a team, a person, a task, from which comes features. Without a good understanding of these relationships, it is impossible to predict outcomes, to suggest completion dates, or even to know what will be delivered. A defined development methodology, coupled with an experienced project manager, will solve these problems. The graph below shows the predominant areas that project management addresses.

Below the Line - 80/20

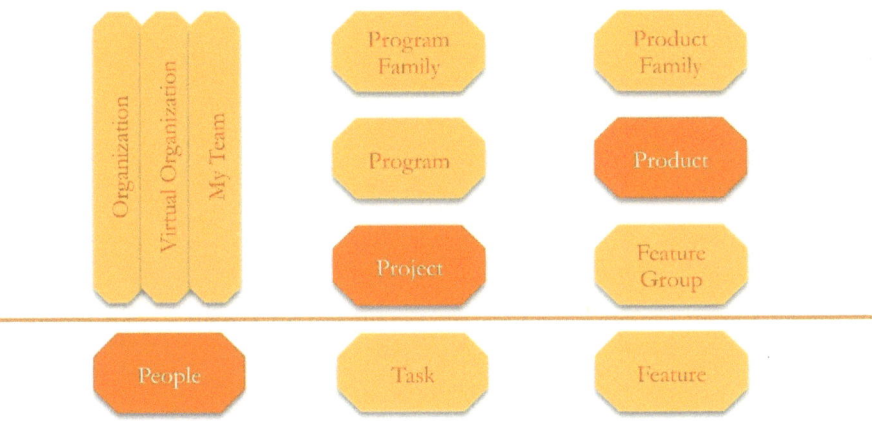

Project management takes into account the other nodes and relationships, but they are not the primary focus. Instead, they serve as a reference to how one project relates to another. Project management involves keeping track of schedules, tasks, reporting, and escalating issues, as well as getting things completed. These functions make up at least 80 percent of the total effort. The other 20 percent comprises attention to the context of and relationship to other projects and products: product structures, how they relate to other products, and how people are allocated to different projects. Project management is below the line.

Portfolio Management—Above the Line

Portfolio management is not about tasks or "getting things done." It is about the whole organization and how all the pieces are put together to maximize the benefits for all. It is not about getting one product out the door or resolving project roadblocks. As such, tasks are not relevant. Instead, the focus is on who is working on what project and the benefits of the effort. "Below the line" is a noisy place. Frequent changes and many data points common to the environment make it very challenging to keep everything up-to-date, especially in larger groups.

Above the Line - 80/20

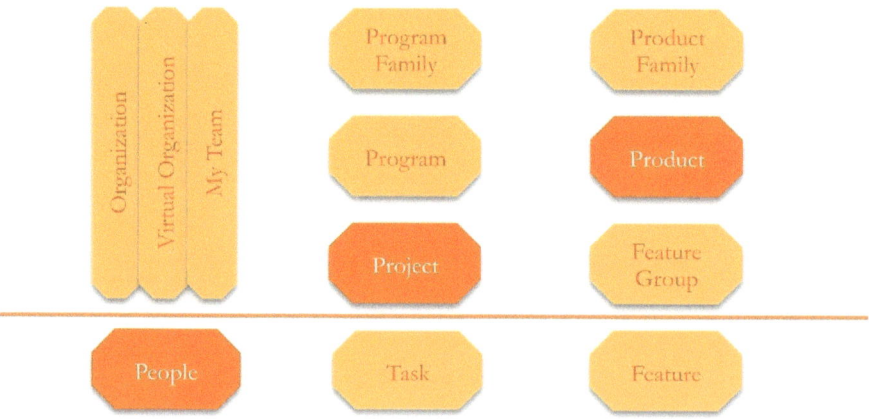

Project-centered information is still accessible, however. By connecting a few data points, it is possible to derive the efforts for every feature. When I have done this in the past, the degree of accuracy has been greater than that achieved using a time-tracking system. In other words, it is possible to extract the cost of product development.

Portfolio management is focused "above the line." Eighty percent or more of activity focuses on how a project contributes to feature groups, products, or product families. The remaining 20 percent involves the features and people.

Above the line is about what you have today and how to make the best use of it. It is about value.

Project management drives tasks; portfolio management drives value.

4

People, Projects and Products

It is now time to leave tasks and organizational structure behind. The focus needs to be on the three "Ps"—people, projects, and products. You can organize these parts in many different ways. Too many types of connections can make it difficult to manage. I will now explore what I believe is a sufficient structure in relation to a company portfolio.

A Different Way of Thinking About a Portfolio

Knowing who is reporting to whom is not critical when managing a portfolio. Instead, product development and the results—the products—are foremost.

One structure is for organizing people and development efforts; the other is for tracking and releasing products. At some point the two structures connect. This connection allows you to then start managing a portfolio that is built around people, projects, and products—the most valuable assets you have.

Portfolio Management

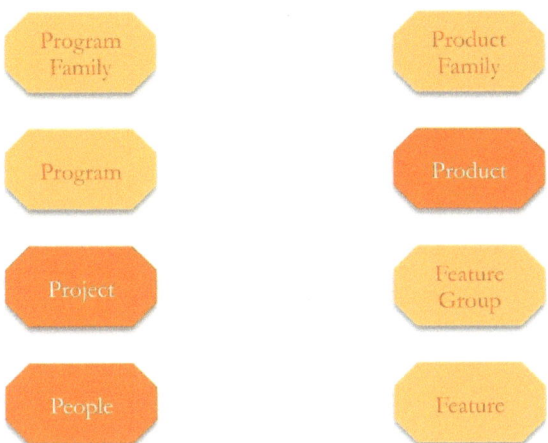

Program Family Structure

There are two types of connections in the program structure. The first is the "one-to-many," connection, which is used to, for example, link a person to projects. Second is the "one-to-one" connection, which is used to attach a project to a program and a program to a program family.

The reason why projects and programs are one-to-one has to do with governance. You cannot have multiple, competing goals and leaders for one effort. You can have a group of leaders working together, but that should be done under the same governance structure—the same project or program. Because a person with specialized skills or expertise might be needed across many projects, it is perfectly fine that one person contributes to more than one project. However, best agile practice suggests that smaller teams stay together and work on one project at a time.

Allocating everyone in the company to one or more projects is the only way to capture the company's total efforts. Not everyone works directly on a product deliverable or a feature, but everyone works on something. I strongly advocate not making a direct connection between people and features because of the ensuing level of noise and the similarity to time tracking. The amount of changes at the feature level is normally very high. When you start assigning people directly to a product, you introduce a fuzzy connection. Nowhere is it captured what a person is doing. All you have is a list of names associated with a product. Using a project, with a named purpose, fills that gap and gives the contribution a name and a purpose. And, as mentioned before, using the product structure as a way of organizing projects is a terrible way of managing efforts. Therefore, link every person to a project. Getting that done in a large organization is in and of itself a big accomplishment.

Projects are efforts big enough to be given a name. They are meant to be easy to create and to update. They should be local to smaller groups, not a company-wide effort. If similar endeavors are taking place in other areas of the company, you should create more projects for those groups. A project is a universal way of organizing and communicating intent. It is a way of showing how people work together around a common goal. A project can have deliverables that directly or indirectly show up in the product structure. Direct deliverables are things such as the backup camera, the bicycle wheel, or the automatic data backup into the cloud. Indirect deliverables are things such as leadership, project management, operations, training and education.

A collection of projects centered on the same purpose should be organized into programs. A program should have an owner; this is key. Without an owner there is no governance, only disparate efforts. You may have a number of people directly supporting a program. In that case, create a project and assign people to that project. Then link that project to the program. Avoid assigning people to a program, as this makes it less clear what a person is working on.

A program typically drives one or more products or services. A program should have a vision, a purpose, a roadmap of future efforts and deliverables, and a governance model that is applied across projects. A program should operate independent of other programs. If needed, you can also organize into families those programs that have some level of interdependency. This can make it a little easier to identify the many efforts across a company.

Product Family Structure

In this structure, there is only one connection type: "many-to-many." For the most part, one feature belongs to one feature group (or component), which, in turn, belongs to one product. Features can be used across many products. In fact, every part of a product should be reusable across many products. In addition, the product structure needs to be flexible to allow the creation of different product flavors to meet customer needs. Products can be bundled in many different ways for sales purposes. Therefore, the product structure needs to be flexible and allow for many-to-many connections.

You may need to break a feature into smaller parts, as it may come from different groups and require some level of assembly. This can be true of both hardware and software. It can be confusing to talk about features that themselves require other features. Organize your product structure in a way that makes sense to you. That might mean having multiple levels of features. But start at the top—begin with a product family and then move down the structure as needed.

A product bundle (not shown on the portfolio graph on page 27) is a collection of products that is brought together for the purpose of selling. A product bundle may consist of several products. There might be small differences to accommodate different types of industry segments. Bundles are part of the portfolio because they tie to revenue and, as such, must then be linked back to the individual products.

People, projects, and products are the core building blocks of portfolio management.

5

Portfolio Management 101

As mentioned in the prior chapter, portfolio management has two main structures. One concerns effort; the other, product. How do the two structures relate to each other? The choices are many, but the graph below shows what I believe will give you the best results without having to move toward time tracking, which is a major investment in any large group.

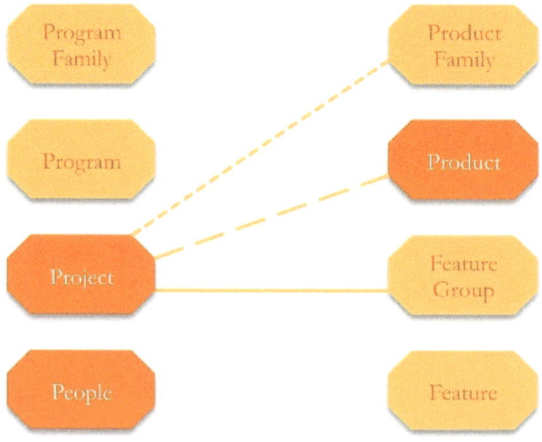

Connecting the Program and Product Structures

As mentioned earlier, there are two types of relationships: one-to-one and many-to-many. In order for a portfolio management system to work, you need to establish relationships between the two structures in the system. Otherwise, you don't know the cost and limitations when developing new products and features.

There are many ways you can approach this; but keep it simple and flexible. Don't aim for perfection. Don't build a system that can't be changed later to address new demands. The more data you require people to enter, the more the organization will push back and the less likely it is that you will end up with the information you were seeking in the first place. In this way, you have trade-offs to make. I will outline here what I have found works well in larger groups.

A project connects to the product structure. The question is, at what level? Suppose you want to track effort at the product level only in order to manage your portfolio. This decision will be OK to start with, but you will quickly see that it is insufficient. How about tracking effort at the feature level? Ideally, that is what you want, but practically speaking this is very tough to do. It simply requires too much data to capture and borders on time tracking. The feature group level is the compromise. It is a unit of measure that an organization seems to be able to deal with. Therefore, the best approach is to connect projects to feature groups.

Creating nodes and making connections requires some effort from everyone in the company. But it is a modest investment. There should be a need to update the content only when there is a change. Everyone should allocate effort to a project. A person should, for the most part, work on one or two projects simultaneously. Certain roles, such as those involving shared resources, may involve working on more projects than others. In those cases, it is useful to establish a minimum allocation such as 5 percent or 10 percent.

Even using this approach, however, you still may end up with projects that are not linked directly to a product or to a product family. You now have choices. You can leave things as they are, and whatever is not allocated is effort that you can show as the cost of running the business. Or you can set up rules for how to distribute these projects across the product structure. For example, you may distribute them equally or pick one product family. Either way, this will enable you to show the overall cost for all of your products.

Managers and senior leaders can create projects called "leadership" and link them to a product family, or they can exclude these projects from the product development cost altogether. The question then becomes more about how you track and report overall research-and-development costs.

The golden rule is that a project must connect to a feature group. Of course, there are other categories, such as the cost of goods sold, that should be attributed to the manufacturing side of the business. But that is not the main focus of portfolio management.

With that in mind, here are the portfolio management tenets in regards to connections:

Area	Recommendations
Program	• A person connects to one or more projects. • A project connects to one program. • A program connects to one program family.
Product	• A feature connects to one or more feature groups. • A feature group connects to one or more products. • A product connects to one or more product families.
Connecting Programs and Products	A project can connect to: • one or more feature groups • one or more products • one or more product families

When you follow this approach, you can allocate the efforts of everyone in product development to a product structure, and, in the process, make it possible to capture the total cost of developing a product.

The lower in the project structure you make the connections, the more accurate the cost numbers will be.

Additional Connections

It is possible to connect programs or program families to the product structure, but this method will not yield the level of detail needed to allow you to make decisions around feature groups or features. You will simply be lumping too many people's efforts into one bucket. Therefore, use this approach only in cases when groups are not able to make a direct connection between their efforts and the feature group. In other words, allocate their projects or programs to a product or product-family level. This approach will allow you to distribute the group's efforts equally across all feature groups and features. Allocating people not directly working on a product becomes overhead or the cost of doing business. The goal is to connect at a lower level of the product structure in order to give you greater insight into making good portfolio decisions.

What About Features?

A portfolio management system should enable you to create and manage features. It should allow linkage to other systems and import all relevant feature information. Most companies use one or more systems to track projects. That information should be linked to the portfolio management system. After connecting the portfolio management system to each of these other tools, you must ask each product or feature group owner to link to features in these systems.

Setting up links to other systems yields extraordinary benefits. It may sound like a lot of work, but it really is not. When I was at Adobe, in one year we developed 150 new features across thirty technologies. This effort was spread across fifteen teams. In that particular case, each team had to link about ten feature groups. The linking itself takes only a few minutes. Is asking a team to invest thirty minutes reasonable? I think so.

At its simplest level, all you need to do is to link features using their name, state, and dates. For example, the feature might be in development with a target completion date. Or the completion date is in the past, and the feature is available for use. Once those links are in place, you can get updates from the other tools. If you don't want to link to a feature directly, you can use search criteria such as naming conventions, prefix or postfix, tags, or states. The latter approach reduces the overhead in managing the links, as you can do most of the work inside the tool where the features are created, meaning outside the portfolio management system.

In order to better track feature development, I suggest establishing a set of feature states such as *Captured, Defined, In Development, Ship-Ready*, and *Shipped*. Another set of states can center around what features to include in the portfolio management tool. You can use something like *Include* or *Not Include*. Why would you allow a team to select what features to include? The answer is, because the early phase of a new technology is fuzzy. There might be a large number of features, or of partially defined or desired features, being evaluated. There is no need to capture these. What is of interest is what teams have gained clarity on, and a simple flag such as *Include* will send that signal. Or, you can bypass that altogether and just use the *Defined* state to indicate that clarity has been achieved.

You may also want to consider setting some guidelines in regard to features. The agile approach requires teams to break down work into small items that can be completed incrementally. Shy away from creating something so big that you don't know when it is done. You can do the same for features. A simple rule is that a feature must fit inside a defined window of time. And this window must not span multiple releases. Break a feature down so it fits inside one release window. If you release every three months, then the duration for developing a feature is at most three months. If you couple this with one more attribute, such as estimation of size, you can do amazing things. A simple large-, medium-, or small-sized estimation is enough, though you can make this more refined if desired. A large-sized estimation would be something requiring ten or more people for more than eight weeks; medium, five people for a month; and small, one to two persons for less than two weeks. You pick.

But you don't have to estimate feature size. You can extract the necessary information from the team size and the development window. If the team comprises, for instance, ten people and the development window is three months, then a large feature will require at most ten people working for three months.

Feature Cost

The amazing part comes next. Assume you have linked your feature groups to features. You know the states of the features, and you have also captured the dates on which these states changed. So if a feature moves from *Defined* to *In Development*, you would know on which date it took place. You would also know when it switched to *Ship-Ready*. Suppose you had a feature that went from *Defined* to *Ship-Ready* in four weeks, and you know who worked on the feature group during that time. You also know what other features were in development during this time window—probably just a handful. So the system could now be set up to calculate the total effort for a feature group for a given period of time. Using a feature-sized estimation to adjust the allocation of efforts yields the best results. In other words, you can easily calculate the total people cost of developing any feature or feature group.

Does this work? Yes, because a team works on only a handful of features at any one time, which provides a very accurate picture. And, certainly for a feature group, you can capture every person's effort and provide the total cost laid out over time. There is simply no more efficient way of capturing the total cost of developing features across a large company.

Roles and Responsibilities

In order to make the portfolio management system work, you have to assign responsibilities for the creation of the nodes and the connections between them. Groups and teams have to agree upon the structure and ownership of the various parts.

I use the generic term "owner" to designate who is responsible for the nodes and connections. As a starting point for this discussion, here are my ownership recommendations for creating nodes and connecting them:

Who	Creates	Connects
Anyone	• Projects	• Own efforts to projects
Project Owner	• Projects	• Projects to programs • Projects to feature groups • If needed, projects to products • If needed, projects to product families
Program Owner	• Programs • Program families	• Programs to program families

Who	Creates	Connects
Product Owner	<ul><li>Features</li><li>Feature groups</li><li>Products</li><li>Product families</li></ul>	<ul><li>Features to feature groups</li><li>Feature groups to products</li><li>Products to product families</li></ul>
Bundle Owner	<ul><li>Product bundles</li></ul>	<ul><li>Products to bundles</li></ul>

You can grant users more than one type of ownership. You may also combine some responsibilities to reduce the number of roles. Either way, the important thing is to have a clear set of rules.

The Connected System Enables Portfolio Management

At this point, you can get a reliable view of your portfolio. You can see who is working on what. You can view all your products in one place. You can roll up total effort for each product viewed over time. This is a great start to creating a framework for portfolio management. In summary, here are some of the key insights the system will reveal by the click of a button:

- What are you working on?
- Who is working on what?
- What are your product structure and list of features?
- What are you shipping today?
- What can you ship at a future date?
- What is the people cost of a project, a program, or a program family for any given period of time?
- What is the people cost of a feature, a feature group, a product, or a product family for any given period of time?

Not all efforts or costs may be allocated to the product structure, but you can now see what is not allocated. You then must decide how to roll up efforts that are not allocated. You can distribute efforts across products, allocate to cost of goods sold, or just leave efforts not allocated to products separate.

Either way, following the approach outlined in this chapter will provide you with a consistent way of calculating development and product costs.

Connecting people, projects, and products enables you to easily answer the basic questions about your portfolio.

6

Portfolio Management 102

So far I have described a model that defines and connects nodes. The nodes are the building blocks and the connections describe how they relate. The benefit of this structure is that you can always introduce more data types at any time without having to change or rebuild the model. The model stays. The additional data types, or attributes, can be anything you want.

Before Adding Attributes

First let's start with some basics. Setting aside the product bundles there are eight nodes in this system. Each one should contain basic information. All which should be searchable. This would allow you to navigate and explore your portfolio. Before adding attributes to nodes and connections there are some key questions to consider.

What else do you have in other systems that should not be connected? For example, you may not want to get all information about every defect (bug) against a product, and every task associated with a person. Rather it may be better to get a summarized data set for bugs and tasks. The filter to apply is what decisions do you want to make versus the cost of getting the data to support those decisions.

The other questions to ponder is what information do you want people to enter directly such as status or priorities. Ask people to enter as little as possible. Only what is needed for important portfolio management decisions. The more information that needs to be entered the less accurate the information becomes. Asking people to keep a large set of data up to date is path that leads to stale information.

Attributes

Nodes and links can contain information entered by a person. You can add analysis and recommendations. You can attach action items to various nodes. Then we have ranking and risks. Ranking is about priorities. Wherever you have priorities you should enter them into the system and attach them to all relevant nodes. Risk is about the unknown. If you can capture risk or the probability of success, enter that too. In some cases it will be easy because you can make your own assessment using simple values such as high, medium or low. In other cases you can instrument your system with statistical analysis and derive risk levels based upon past data in your portfolio management system.

Categories of Attributes

Among the eight nodes, there are three major types: people, projects and products. In this case product also extends to product families, feature groups, and features. The project extends to programs and program families. Each has a set of attributes such as name, age, gender, height and weight. Not quite. But you get the point. Make your own list. My list will include items such as numeric identifier, name, description, creation date, last update date, close date, owners with roles, and links to more data. But to start the basic set of attributes for each of them could be:

- People: role, job, location, skills, salary, etc.
- Project: description, purpose, owners, type, etc.
- Product: description, purpose, owners, benefits, ship-ready state, etc.

For a person it is useful to capture the job description and the role. The role should not be added to the person node, but rater to a project node where the name could be listed under owner role for example. Type of employee might be useful such a full time, part time contractor, vendor, etc.

In a company there is a large number of job ladders and levels. All of this info should be made available in the system, brought over from the organizational system of records. It useful to create summary categories such as software developer, technical writer, program manager, etc. and filter all job categories via this lens. It makes it much easier to understand the composition of projects and efforts behind delivering new features.

For a project I would add the state of the project such an experiment, starting out, established, or placed into maintenance. I would do the same for features, feature groups and products.

Where possible you should link to other systems that have supporting data. For example, the organizational structure should come from the core IT systems. Salaries and other describing data about employees should be linked in as well. Sales should link in their actual sales, booking and forecasting to the product bundles. Support should link in their support data to the product structure, at feature level if possible. Localization can use the product structure to show their schedules and cost tracking. You can use bug reporting (defects) and link that data to feature groups to get insight into the level of quality and the level of effort still required to become ship-ready.

Ranking – The Importance of Things

There are two types of ranking relevant to portfolio management – absolute and relative. The absolute ranking depends upon a predefined set of measures. The relative ranking depends upon the context in which it is measured. For example revenue for a product is absolute. You can measure each product and make a list ranked from first to last. Or it can be a list of priorities as defined by management such as areas to invest in. Sometimes it makes sense to do a local absolute ranking. This could be the revenue rank for all products in a business segment.

Another way of ranking products is to create buckets. Products in a company can be placed into categories such as flagship, upcoming, stable or new. Flagship is what drives the revenue. Upcoming is the next group that has yet to see the revenue growth. Stable are those products that make money, but are not driving growth. They are typically a magnitude lower as compared to flagship. New is untested products that will need some time to be validated or retired.

A relative ranking is dependent upon context. An example of a relative ranking is the importance of a feature for a specific product. For one product it can be the number one selling feature, while for another product it can be a nice to have feature.

Similarly, feature groups depend upon the product they are linked to. In some products they are less important, while in others, they are they main selling points. So feature groups may be ranked within their product using a simple high, medium and low.

Regardless of the type or ranking, almost every item in the portfolio should have meaningful rank assigned. It does not have to be an absolute rank from 1 to 100. It can be placed into a few categories. For example, how critical is this defect or bug. Does it create data loss? If so, rank it 1. If it is a small cosmetic issues that does not impact functionality or confuses the user, then rank it 5. It can be ranking at a component or feature group level. How important is this group of features to a product? Does it drive the key use cases and is why the customers buy? If so rank it a 1. Is it a group of features that enable you to connect to another application for some type of esoteric file format that almost nobody uses? Then rank it a 5.

Some things will be easy to rank such as bugs. Ranking bug impact is baked into the development and test discipline. In other areas ranking will feel more foreign as it is normally not done, and often you may lack data to justify the ranking. It will be up to the portfolio owners to decide what will be ranked and how. The thing to remember is that ranking is way of communicating priorities to simplify decision-making across the company.

In the absence of clear company priorities groups will use their own priorities. In my opinion it is better to have a simple and low-key way of assigning them than to have nothing at all. Use High, Medium and Low (or 1, 2 and 3). Ask people who are responsible for projects, products or groups to make these assessments. It should be relatively easy for a project team to take their own product and break it into feature groups and rank them 1, 2 or 3.

Drop Status Reporting to Get Status

Status reporting is a complicated topic in product development. It surfaces immediately when talking about projects or even portfolio management. Some groups demand every person write a detailed status every week. Others ask for nothing. The reason we want status reports is to understand what is going on and trying to predict impact of what is done or and what is not done. A project management system is focused on tasks and as such provides much of the status needed for driving a project forward. In the portfolio management view the status needed is more about the state of the system itself. What do we have? What can be shipped? What are we doing that perhaps need to change to get better results?

You can get much of this data by adding a time stamp to every change in the system. Every time a node is updated or a connection is changed, the system should capture the current set of data, and the date and time of the change. This forms the foundation for system-generated information. For example, John changed his percentage effort toward one project. Instead he contributed to another project. A new project was added. A new person joined the company. A product shipped. You can also link other data points to the nodes such as number of bugs in a particular state; and test coverage achieved for a given product. The list can be endless.

You can now gain insight into the system in ways you could not do before. For example, you can view list of projects created the last week or new people added to a project. You can view what features have change states and moved into ship-ready. You can view the recently added products or modified feature groups. You can see how many products are using your favorite feature. You can view how many people were contributing to your product on daily basis. The list goes on. Every change in the system if captured can be used to better understand your product development efforts.

If this is implemented the system itself will be able to present you with status or views of what has changed from week to week or any time period you choose. This in essence becomes what's new or your status report. This approach allows you direct information into what is taking place in the company without anyone needing to report status. Or filter the meaning of what is taking place. This is the escape from Alcatraz. This is how you get out of prison. This is how you get in touch with life in the city.

Analysis and Recommendations

Having said all this some level of analysis added to projects or products still have value. It is prudent to consider asking teams to provide a brief summary or list of issues. However, this information should not be in a separate system. It should be capture next to the project. For example, a project in the system could have "what's new." Of course, you could extract all of them into a central report. But use this reporting lightly to avoid the system being seen as a project-tracking tool.

Every project could have action items. This is someone's assessment of issues or opportunities around specific topics. For example, the project could have a number of feature gaps that should be addressed. But don't overuse this opportunity. This is a portfolio management system, not a project management solution.

Every node can have additional information added by a person. A person, a project, a program, a feature or a product can have an informational field. You can make this a text field or a list of various states such as I'm OK or I need help. You can then view this by date, by product, or by program.

Depending upon what you are comfortable with you can add information to everything or pick a few items. I would make this as lightweight as possible. No personal status reports. Focus on efforts, such as projects. Each project could have a brief one-paragraph summary of events on a weekly basis. In addition, I would capture information for feature groups and products to understand their ship-ready state and any upcoming releases. But not much more.

Adding attributes to your portfolio opens the door to unlimited insight into your portfolio. It allows you to escape from Alcatraz and join life in the city.

7

Decision Making

Consider the game of poker. In order to assess your chances of winning a particular hand, you have to remember what cards have already been played. If an ace has been played and you are holding three, there is no chance you will get a fourth—assuming there are no wild cards. But you may be able to get two fours, resulting in a full house. Based upon the risk and the possible return, you place your bets and play your hand or fold. Portfolio optimization is the same—it is about evaluating risks and returns, about playing or folding.

At its core, portfolio optimization is about decision making. How do you select a course of action between two or more alternatives? The goal is to get the best outcome. It is about selecting where to invest time, money, and resources to optimize revenue, happy customers, and great products.

Preferences

Suppose a friend offered you a choice of ice cream: vanilla or chocolate. You decided on the chocolate. The uncertainty of the outcome was low. Either choice would have gotten you what was offered. In other words, the uncertainty was nil. This choice was based only upon your preferences. This makes decision making easy. You know what you want and the outcome is certain. If only everything were this easy!

Probability

Now, imagine you were offered the opportunity to buy a share in a company. You have two companies to choose from, A or B. Each has a share price worth $100. The best analysts said that stock A would reach $120 by year's end. They also predicted stock B would reach $200 in the same time period. This seems like a straightforward decision. Let's look at return on investment.

Stock A: ($120-$100) = $20
Stock B: ($200-$100) = $100

Let's go for stock B! But wait. What are the chances that either prediction will be accurate? How do you assess this? You could look back at how accurate the analysts were at predicting stock prices in the past. Or you could do some research on your own. Let's say, after thorough research, you estimated that there was a 50 percent chance that stock A would reach its target price, a 25 percent chance it would reach $110, and a 25 percent chance that it would stay at $100. For stock B, you projected that there was a 10 percent chance that it would reach $200, a 50 percent chance that it would reach $150, and a 40 percent chance that it would drop to $50. Now let's compare the expected returns.

Stock A: $20*0.5 + $10*0.25 + $0*0.25 = $12.5
Stock B: $100*0.1 + $50*.05 +(-50)*0.4 = $5

Of course, this is an oversimplification of possible outcomes. The point is that the outcome of a decision can be divided into defined categories that cover all possible outcomes. And each can be assigned a probability of occurring. The sum of these probabilities must add up to one, the sum of all possible outcomes.

When dealing with outcomes associated with flipping a coin or tossing the dice, the possible outcomes are easy to determine. This is not the case when you have real-life choices where the outcomes are many, and perhaps some of them are unknown. But having a framework that captures probability will help drive better decision making.

The Decision-Making Basement

In the above examples, there are two things going on. In the first case, you made a decision by using your own preferences for ice cream flavors. You might not have been able to articulate it in detail, but you do have an internal list called "My Top Ice Cream Flavors." You took a look your list and made your decision. The risk of not getting what you desired was negligible and, hence, was ignored.

In the second case, the outcome was uncertain. So you had to look for information to make guesses or predictions about the future. You did this by assigning numerical values to the different outcomes.

In both cases, these decisions were made in the basement. Nobody else was privy to your ranked lists or predictions. In order to make good portfolio-optimization decisions, it is critical that these are moved out of the basement and made visible for all to see long before a choice is to be made. You can accomplish this by capturing rank and risk information in your portfolio management system.

Preferences and Probabilities

Portfolio optimization is about preferences and risks. Another way of thinking about preferences is to use the word *priorities*. How important is a set of tasks? What are the key features as measured by frequency of use? What are the areas of investment you (or management) have selected for the company? Every object in a portfolio can be ranked from top to bottom, or, more practically, in buckets such as high, medium, and low or from one to five.

Risk is about what comes next—the unknown. Given a particular situation, what is the likelihood that an event will take place? For example, if you have a choice of developing feature A or feature B, which one would you select? If the product has one hundred open bugs, what is the likelihood that a customer will find any of them? And what then are the expected customer support costs?

The biggest problem with risk is that it is difficult to determine the level using a quantitative approach. Very often, risk level is derived from someone's experience. If you have been working in an area for a while, you easily recognize things that you are comfortable with and that you think will go well. On the flip side, we have all seen dysfunctional projects and, as a result, we assume that their outcomes will not be good.

In the case of evaluating a project, you may be able to assess its level of risk by using a project team maturity level. In other words, you can compare a particular team's behavior with factors that are common to most well-performing teams. This does not necessarily appraise the quality of the deliverables accurately, but it certainly provides an overall assessment of the project team's ability to produce predictable results.

If you have an established way of estimating risks, then use it. It can be based upon a set of factors as defined by you. Think about your past experience in product development and make a list of successful projects. What do they have in common? Then use this list to evaluate the capabilities of all your current projects. If you assign them a label or value, you have now added a risk factor to your projects. Is this easy to do? Yes. Will people feel uncomfortable with the risk value? Yes—if you do the ranking. But if you share the information and ask teams to compare themselves to the factors, you will have far fewer issues to deal with.

Of course, this does not work when assessing a product feature's success rate in the marketplace. That requires a different approach that may rely on market research or a comparison of prior successful features against new ones.

How and when you can apply risk will vary. But having options available for all elements in the portfolio is what makes calculating returns or portfolio optimization possible.

Determining Probabilities Using Your Own Data

Another way of assessing risk is to examine past and current data. Look for correlations among data sets. Do a number of open issues at some point in the development of a product point to a higher risk of not completing a feature as planned? Does the number of changes to a feature indicate that the quality level will be better or worse?

While I was at Apple—a time of waterfall projects—the company was trying to understand what would enable a project team to deliver a quality product, on schedule, with all the promised features. A small group of us were looking to introduce a product development lifecycle that was designed for success: one that had the right best practices and the best incentives and that led to innovative products. After a year of looking into every past project we could find, we arrived at our conclusion. A successful project could be predicted by five attributes, which were recorded in well-written documents. The attributes were: a marketing requirements document, an engineering requirements specification, a project plan, a quality plan, and test plans. Those projects that produced these documents as planned were by far much more likely to achieve success. As a result, we introduced the "key-doc" initiative, which formed the basis of the product development lifecycle, named ANPP—Apple New Product Process. This approach allowed us to assign project risk based upon the presence and completeness of these documents or the lack thereof.

It is possible to extract a wide range of formulas based upon your own data set. A statistician can run your data through statistical analysis and make recommendations. The problem is not a lack of useful correlations, but rather the volume of them. So you have to select a few that are relevant and have the most impact. At VMware I was lucky enough to work with a data analyst. It was amazing how much past development data could be used to predict future states of projects. Looking at bugs and when they were resolved, it was possible to predict if a project would meet a future deadline. It was also possible to predict the level of bug escapes and therefore the cost of support.

"Big Data" is a term referring to large data sets that may be analyzed to reveal patterns and trends related to human behavior. It is often used for websites and applications. If you have access to "big data," you can link this to your portfolio management system at the feature or product level and use it for indicating preferences or risks. This can become a powerful tool for providing product and customer insight.

Since we are dealing with teams, we also have to consider the human factor. The data may suggest that a project will be late because of the number of open bugs. But if you know that several team members will soon return from an extended vacation—meaning that team capacity will grow in the near future—your concern may dissipate. Therefore, always look for the human factor behind the data before making any decision.

Decision Making and Product Development

Here is a typical question: Should you add more people to a project wanting to add a new big feature? Before answering this question, you may want to look at why this request was put forth. Why is the feature needed? Do you need more people to add more valuable features? Is the product quality not where it needs to be? What happens if you don't add anybody? What are the returns and the risk in this scenario? If we are agile, why not develop this feature later? Regardless of the reason, there will be times when promises have been made and time is running out. Here are some questions that a project team should consider before making a request to add more people:

- Is it important that we deliver this new feature? If we are adding a person, what is the new ship date? If we are not adding a person, what is the new ship date? Can we live with the delta in time?
- Does the gap in staffing mean we lack the expertise to build the product? And, as a result, might we not be able to solve a customer problem?
- Will the decision to not add a person result in lower quality?

When you start adding the portfolio lens, a number of new factors come into play and you get a broader view of all the other parts of the portfolio. Here are some new questions that arise via the portfolio lens:

- How important is this project as compared to all the others being worked on in the company? Is it ranked #2 or #23?
- Does the project support a product that is mature and will soon be retired?
- Will any of the features cause the product to not be shipped as planned and have an impact on revenue? What is the risk of losing or delaying revenue?
- How does the postponement of a feature's shipping affect the overall customer experience?
- What is the chance that adding a person will make anything change? Often, adding a person who is not familiar with the product mid-cycle has the opposite effect of what was intended—and makes things worse in the short run.
- What is the expected return? Is it reasonable?
- Are there other places to invest where the returns are better and the risk lower?

Both sets of assessments should be made. The project teams should drive the answers to these questions to ensure they meet their committed goals. They should have complete access to data at all levels of the portfolio. This makes it simpler for everyone, provides transparency—and improves the speed and quality of decision making.

One more thing about decision making. It is perfectly fine to delay it because you need more data or you can make the choice later without impacting the outcome. Knowing when a decision needs to be made is as important as making it. A decision that is made too late can have no impact on the result. A decision that is made too early might not be based on important information that could have changed it. The problem is that sometimes you don't know what the best timing is. In that case, the solution is to monitor progress and make new decisions as needed to course correct.

Schedules

Here are two often-asked questions: Is the product ready to ship? Will the new set of features ship as planned on the given date? If the project is in a good state and you expect little or no changes, you may be able to say that you will be ready to ship. In other words, you deferred from the level of change that the success rate was so high that no risk assessment needed to be done. On the other hand, if the project has many open issues and you are expecting more changes, you may be less certain of which direction to go in.

How do you assess risk levels or the chances that the project will ship as planned? One approach is to compare your project to others that are in a similar situation. For example, look at defects or bugs. You may compare them to a prior version of your own product or to someone else's product. If they followed a similar development methodology, you can start assessing the rate of finding new bugs and of closing open bugs. It is possible to do a statistical analysis and find correlations between the phase of a project and the likelihood that you will reach a future date with a particular number of open defects.

Let's say in your case a statistician had instrumented the portfolio management tool with this data. You ran the analysis and found that the chance of meeting your ship date with the desired bug level was 50 percent. Probably your first reaction is to question the number. How was it calculated? Is it accurate? What is the error range for this calculation? Once you get these answers, you'll then look at the numbers and probably not like the odds. What should you do? Let's look at some options.

Eliminate the Schedule Risk

The promise of the agile approach is that you never have to be in a position where you are at risk of not being on schedule, as your product is always shippable. You can always ship what you have. You may not have what you need and, therefore, will not ship. In this situation, there are other issues that might be more relevant than determining a future ship date. One question you must address is what the expected value of your current set of new features is as compared to the cost of the release? You can break this down further and ask, what is the probability that this release will increase sales or hit the current planned sales level? This question requires more data in regard to what type of features you are releasing and what occurred in the case of other products that were in similar situations.

One case is easy. Suppose you fixed a random set of bugs and added a minor feature that deals with error handling. Few would want to upgrade or purchase this feature. But what if you added a great feature that really made your product simpler to use; would it sell more? A simple way of determining this could be through a competitive comparison. Is this feature behind, at par, or ahead of the competition? If you were behind and this brings you at par, the sales would probably not jump. It may just stay as is or at least not fall behind. If it brings you well ahead of the competition, perhaps you could see a sales increase. You can now assign a probability that you can reach a certain incremental sales increase based upon the category of the feature. If this increase outweighs the cost of a release, you now have an opportunity to justify a release.

Of course, the cost of a release should include the engineering effort to review, test, and deliver the product. It should cover marketing costs, training costs for support groups, legal review costs, the cost of filing patents, etc. And it should include future costs that might be incurred by the development groups, such as extended compatibility testing or a more complex install or upgrade logic that needs to be developed. If possible, make a return-on-investment (ROI) assessment before a feature is approved for development in the first place to better plan out a release schedule.

Preferences and Probabilities—Add Them to the Portfolio

There are many questions that development teams face on a daily basis. In order to help teams make decisions quickly with good guidance, the portfolio management system should be set up to provide as much directional data as possible. Therefore, make it clear what is important and what is less important. Clarify what is high risk and what is not. This level of transparency can make leaders nervous because of the concern that such visible priorities will offend people. Nobody wants to know that his or her efforts are considered less important than someone else's.

But, let's face it. By not being transparent, you are misleading your teams. You are allowing them to go in directions that are less critical than those that are really important. My experience is that people can handle the truth. They understand direct and honest communication. In fact, they will thank you! Everyone knows that trade-offs have to be made. Sometimes people come out ahead; sometimes they don't. But understanding how decisions are made will make a world of difference. In fact, it will encourage teams to seek out guidance in everything they do so that they can support the company. Everyone wants to make a positive impact. Let them! Allow them to be guided by the information in the portfolio management system. The system should always reflect the collective best information everyone has about the state of development and about what is and is not important.

Make transparent decision making a core part of portfolio management.

8

Portfolio Optimization

A quick recap: *portfolio management* is the place where requirements of customers, partners, and stakeholders come together with product development teams to ensure creation of roadmaps with all the right product capabilities at the right time. The measure of portfolio success is maximized return for a given level of risk – also called *portfolio optimization.*

In the words of Jefferson "In any moment of decision, the best thing you can do is the right thing, the next best thing is the wrong thing, and the worst thing you can do is nothing."

Optimization

Optimization is like balancing on a tightrope. It is about moving from here to there without falling. You have to slow down and carefully decide which way to lean to avoid falling. In the real world sometimes that means investing in growing market share over revenue growth. Sometimes it means building a few great products versus many that are not.

When optimizing a portfolio you may have to do all of these and more at the same time. Therefore you need to capture different views of data in the system to allow you to analyze and think about the challenges in different ways. For example, what is current set of priorities across projects ranked from first to last? What is the number one problem reported by a customer? Should you invest more in customer support and less in development? How much effort to set aside for speculative, highly risky projects versus revenue certain projects?

Not Optimization

Say you implemented a new tool that saved every person who used it 10 minutes per week. If this tool was used in a group of 200 people, this equates to a savings over a year to about 10,000 minutes or 42 weeks. This is close to one-person year worth of effort. What could this be used for? Answer: nothing. The truth is that we don't function like machines. We operate on human time where 10 minutes is not a currency we can deposit into a secure location.

On the other hand if the tool removed the need to have a dedicated support group of five people then you might be able to allocate that team to something new. Of course you have to subtract the cost of the tool to calculate your cost savings.

Here is another not portfolio optimization path. If you have a choice of making one manager feel important by granting him or her resources for their own pet projects versus investing in the new direction of the company do the right thing. Say no. Don't allow special interest to torpedo company interests. You will see disastrous results placating selfish leaders.

The Future

You can use data about past and current behavior in your company and the market place to predict outcomes. You should compare all predicted outcomes to allow you to make decisions to optimize the short and long term value of your portfolio of products and technologies.

The challenge is of course having the discipline and patience to get to this point. It takes time and effort. Should you choose to invest in getting here you are truly free from the prison walls. You have climbed the prison walls and can enjoy the view from the tower. You can view land above the fog. You can see the sun breaking though. Your can glimpse what will come.

Portfolio optimization is running the company and therefore the responsibility of company leadership.

9

The Idea Showcase

New ideas are critical to success. A key part of portfolio management is to evaluate new ideas, new features, and new products. Taking an idea and making it into a product is a challenge. But if you structure the path, it can make the journey easier and give you more innovation within your current portfolio limits.

In California, the area between San Francisco and San Jose—often referred to as Silicon Valley—is a magical place. The availability of investor money, entrepreneurial spirit, and high-tech expertise, as well as a wide customer base, makes it the envy of the world. Visitors want to replicate it in their own cities. Many countries have invested large amounts of money in building their own versions, or they have sent companies or representatives to Silicon Valley to take part in the adventure. Often they expect the path to be straightforward: make a list, mix the ingredients, and reap the reward. I have been there, engaging with governmental representatives and local companies. What was most surprising to me were their expectations. Visitors would rightfully point out that their ideas or technologies were better than anyone else's in the world. They met with leading companies. They were ready to conquer the world. But yet, it did not happen. Why?

The same thing takes place within an organization. A company's Silicon Valley happens to be where the money and the decision makers are. Everyone in the company wants to put forth an idea in the hope of becoming successful.

The root of the problem is that good ideas are not scarce; they are everywhere. Everybody knows something that can change the future. The problem is implementation and competition. Success requires relentless effort and dedication. It requires sacrifice. Even then, success is not certain.

There are countless individuals and companies who have become successful. How did they do it? There are books written about them. There are books written about becoming an entrepreneur and how to build innovative companies. If you know of an approach that works, use it. Experiment with different approaches. Some may fail. But keep trying—it is the attempt that will make all the difference. With that in mind, let's try something new.

Every corporation has untapped potential. How can you use the best ideas? Let me give you a path for connecting ideas to portfolio management. This connection will not replace the need for insight and good decision making. But, it gives an idea a voice. It provides a platform from which to draw data that will help you understand its potential.

Innovation

Before we go on, let's pause a second to ponder the word *innovation*. It is a big word. It has many meanings. It has been used in many different ways at every level of a company. There are published lists of the "most innovative companies in the world." So, what is innovation? Some say it is a new method, idea, or product—something we have not seen before. Others say it is a process. What, then, is innovation? I would like to keep it simple. I will define innovation as *the development and market introduction of a new or improved product or service.*

Innovation Challenges

When faced with the opportunity to invest in a new idea, you hedge your bets. You look at the risks and returns, and you compare the idea against other types of investments. In the absence of strong indications of success, you are hesitant. In a corporation, there are many forces that push back on great ideas.

A company can be successful and considered inventive without having an articulated strategy for innovation. There are many companies that build great products that solve customers' problems. They have a laser focus.

They make decisions that bring them closer to their goals. They value innovation. They want innovation.

The innovation challenge is similar to the portfolio challenge. There is typically no company-wide framework for discussing how to go about innovation in the most efficient way and tap into and evaluate ideas. What you normally see are different groups fending for themselves. They adopt their own approach. Sometimes leaders even encourage internal competition, with the expectation that the best idea will win out. As a result, achieving collaboration across groups is very difficult, as each member has different priorities and different ways of thinking about innovation.

You may see company-wide initiatives that encourage innovation. Organizations might offer training or hold events where teams can present their ideas and get rewarded. Some companies arrange "hack-a-thons," where developers get together to create new software solutions within days. All of these are good things. But is there an articulated strategy that makes it clear what the path is for a new idea? If there is, has anyone taken this road and achieved success? Even if an idea follows a stated strategy, it might not work well enough to warrant investing in to begin with.

What happens when someone in a company comes along with a great new idea that is far beyond anything that has already been attempted? The idea owner loves the idea and wants to make it a reality. But the rest of the organization has no experience with or insight into this area. For example, say that you developed a software product that made editing photos easy for professional photographers. Then someone else has an idea for how to make it easier for students to submit their homework online. Both are software solutions, but the potential customers are miles apart. What is the chance that a developer who understands photographers also understands students? The person with an idea that is far outside the company norm will have a steeper hill to climb. Should we encourage this? Maybe, but we should agree that his or her chance of success is lower than that of a person whose ideas are within the realm of the company's core competencies.

An approach that is likely to be less successful is an idea that requires the development of a totally new product. The level of investment needed for a new product is significantly higher than that that would be required for adding a new feature to a current product. Does this mean you should not invest in new products? No! It just means that that you should be aware of the cost and risks when doing so.

Let's imagine a team puts forth an idea that requires a reasonable level of investment and that from the outset appears to augment your current product portfolio. What should your next move be?

Major Milestones

Based upon my own experience, most ideas get stuck at one of three milestones that every new idea has to reach. They are:

1. Concept validation
2. Functionality validation
3. Productization

Most new ideas are fueled by the motivations of the innovators. Most ideas die because they do not have enough support and resources to prepare for the above milestones. Most new innovators grossly underestimate the effort it requires to arrive at these milestones. Instead, they prefer to go straight into the customer's open arms.

The first problem a new idea meets is concept validation. How do you know that this new product or service will work? Who are the customers? Will they be willing to pay for it? Will it be worth the effort? Unless someone has done this before or has the support of an experienced team, this is where most ideas fade. It seems simple. The idea sounds good. Why would it not work? Getting to the core of the message requires several iterations and fine-tuning. Can the idea be described in thirty seconds or less? If not, why? If it takes thirty minutes or longer to state the core of the idea, that is an indication of rambling. Has the idea been presented to different groups or stakeholders who have provided feedback? Is there evidence that can back up this specific idea? Don't use general statements such as, "Health care will grow 30 percent over the next five years." Concept validation takes time and effort. It is about building a shared mindset and making the idea come alive based upon its own merits.

Let's imagine the idea has been validated. There is a core message that can be stated in thirty seconds or less. There is support from many different groups. There are details on how the idea can be morphed into a product. Now, is there a way of validating that it will work? Will the new product function as planned and will potential customers react in a way that will cause them to want to use it? What will they pay for this new product? At this point you have to provide a near-functional prototype, something that resembles the final product. This is normally more costly than validating the concept. It requires more people, more time, and more money to build. It should not be built to last; it should be built to validate. Sometimes this can be done on paper; sometimes it requires an almost completed product. Either way, it has to be done.

Let's say the functionality has been validated. There is still one more milestone. Will the idea be funded to make it into a product? Is someone willing to finance this idea as compared to another idea? Will the idea result in a product that is successful enough to make it worth the investment? This decision must be based on a comparison of this idea to other ideas and current products. This is a portfolio decision. New ideas face a lot of competition. Competition is normal. Expect it to happen and be prepared for it!

Innovation Strategy

Now, take the innovation challenges and turn them upside down. Instead of letting ideas die in the quagmire of organizational inefficiency, make them flourish. Grease the skids; make it almost impossible to miss a good idea that has been validated and that has the ROI to compete with other efforts under way at the company. Make innovation a core part of doing business.

Create a strategy. Make it possible for good ideas to be validated and placed into production. Don't miss out on getting great ideas for free. Seek out those that augment the existing product line. Encourage ideas that the company can validate and support. Set expectations. Let everyone know what is possible.

Make it clear what the company can support and what it cannot. Let employees know what products and technologies can be supported. Let them know which areas will not be supported. There is nothing worse than a large number of employees looking to get their idea funded and finding nothing but closed doors. Don't lead them into the desert. That is a recipe for disaster. Morale will plummet.

First, a company should decide how much it wants to invest in different types of projects. For example, what percentage should be allocated to flagship products, to new and upcoming products that have yet to make it big, and to totally new product ideas? Normally a company invests the most in the first two categories and perhaps only 5 to 10 percent in new product ideas. And, for the most part, these new product ideas are aligned with its current core competency. Either way, it is important to make a decision on this investment profile and communicate it in order to set expectations.

Second, there should be guidance available on expected success rates. For example—again based upon my own experience—here is a ranked list of the success rate of new ideas, from high to low:

1. Ideas that enhance the current product line within your team or scope of influence.
2. Ideas that enhance the current product line but outside of your group.
3. Ideas that require a new product within the current product line.
4. Ideas that require a new product outside of the current product line.

Use the Community to Validate Innovation

A major problem with new ideas is that they have to go through a number of groups or people who do not have time to review them. Therefore, ideas stall. Instead, build a system that does not involve one particular person's assessment. Let the community speak. Let the world speak up; gather feedback from users or anyone interested. If the community ranks a concept high, let them interact with the solution. Gather more feedback. Let them again speak up. If they like it, then move on to seeking feedback from individuals within the organization who have decision-making authority. The more broadly you reach out to the world, the better chance you have for getting ideas heard.

Provide support for the ideas that the community likes. If they meet stated criteria, support the ideas through the milestones. Use the community to validate innovation rather than a small group or a few individuals.

New ideas are like seedlings. Don't block the sun. Step aside and let them grow.

10

Your Leadership Opportunity

If you were to follow and implement the concepts in this book, you would have created something amazing. You would have built a system and a discipline that captures everyone's best knowledge about the company portfolio. And this information would be current, as it is linked to other systems and people's everyday activities. The system would be able to provide historical data that would allow you to capture and to recognize trends. It would have built-in predictive indicators to help you make better decisions. The wealth of knowledge at your fingertips would open doors that could lead you to new and amazing places. The ability to make all this real-time information available to anyone would be so powerful that it would change the organization.

You may have many of the necessary parts of this system. However, there is a possibility that you have a not implemented it as outlined in this book. Perhaps you have been able to create a similar system using a combination of files and tools. With that in mind, let's review your most likely situation:

- You may have access to data about everything you are currently doing in your company.
- You may be able connect this data to what matters to you, such as cost, strategic priorities, and market opportunities.
- You may be able to apply data about past and current behavior in your company and in the marketplace to predict outcomes.

- You may be able to compare all of the predicted outcomes in order to make decisions that would optimize the short- and long-term value of your portfolio of products and technologies.
- You may be able to do all of this anytime you want without asking anyone to do anything.

That is quite a few maybes. But herein lies the gold. Regardless of what you have today, this is where you have to start. Anything new always begins with someone envisioning a different future, someone challenging the status quo, someone willing to take the first step. That someone can be you!

The chance to turn a maybe into reality is your opportunity!

What you do have is a blueprint. Armed with this knowledge, you are in a situation where you understand what is possible. You can make portfolio management become real by asking questions. You can make teams aware of what you are looking for. You can lead the organization toward portfolio thinking. If you keep at it, systems and solutions will eventually be enhanced to better answer your questions. You may even see new solutions being procured to fill gaps in the portfolio tool space. But without a leader, this opportunity will be lost.

Where to Start?

You can start anywhere. Insert questions in any meeting or event. It can be as simple as, "What will happen if we don't ship this feature as promised, but instead wait until it's going to make customers happy? Will we really lose sales in the long run?" You may not get the answer you want, but you will get the conversation started.

When a group asks to hire another engineer, ask, "What difference will this make? Will it be more important than hiring a new manager for the group or spending more on marketing?"

When your group enters a planning phase, ask what key values will be used to evaluate current and new investments. How do you then compare them? Does each team evaluate its own, or do you review them across larger groups?

Ask questions when new systems and solutions are being improved or introduced for the first time. For example, you can ask if the feature tracking system will connect with the people tracking system. If it doesn't, suggest that it needs to. The data models might be different, but a new one can be created that will allow the systems to be connected. And the list goes on.

Show the Way

Moving toward portfolio management requires making changes across every team, functional group, and system. This will take time, and it will require you to display leadership every day. Create visual images of what you want to see. Start communicating in terms of relative priorities, ranking, and risks. Insert your ideas in every possible place where decisions about people, money, or resources are made. Show that you understand the overall portfolio in your group or company. Encourage others to do the same. Demand that everyone works to support what is best for the company, and do not allow smaller teams to optimize their own worlds on the backs of others. Local optimization that hurts the company is a clear signal that leaders lack understanding of portfolio optimization.

Remove the Walls

Let's return to Alcatraz. Leading a large corporation is like being behind prison walls. You have limited access to real-time data, and most of it is filtered through slow and unreliable channels.

Hopefully, this book has shown you how to break down the walls and how to implement a portfolio management system. But, most importantly, I hope it has shown you how to think about product development and how to manage the innovation machine.

Getting out of prison might not be accomplished through a carefully planned escape, but rather by tearing down the walls brick by brick to allow the people inside to slowly start to see the city. And as the bustling life of the city starts to emerge, they will also understand that they need new skills and tools to be successful. In other words, by showing what is possible, people will naturally see the importance of portfolio optimization.

Behave as if portfolio optimization is the only way to run a successful company—and it will be.

About the Author

Erik Boe is currently working at VMware, where he defines and implements portfolio management and software delivery models. Prior to that he was at Adobe, where he was part of a global technology group that delivered technologies to all Adobe product teams. This central and unique position enabled him to gain deep insight into technology portfolio management and innovation across the company. Before joining Adobe, he was with a startup that was struggling to deliver Internet storage solutions.

His career began at Apple, where he worked before, during, and after the company's turnaround—first in the MacOS group and later in the hardware division. His roles ranged from software engineer to manager and program manager, and he drove company-wide efforts focused on optimizing technology delivery and innovation.

He holds a master's degree in international business from Pepperdine University and a bachelor of computer science degree from the University of California, Santa Barbara.

He grew up in Norway and later moved to California to join the personal computer revolution. He currently lives in California, with his wife, three children, a dog, and a cat.

www.ingramcontent.com/pod-product-compliance
Lightning Source LLC
Chambersburg PA
CBHW040835180526
45159CB00001B/199